Succeeding with 5S

WCM Consulting AB is a consulting company that supports the introduction of Lean and World Class Manufacturing

Feel free to contact the author at:

oskar@world-class-manufacturing.com

Read more at www.world-class-manufacturing.com/

Thank you
Thank you to Daniel Adolfson, Mattias Brodén, Anna-Carin Söderlund, Cornel Oancea and Stefan Olofsson

Image sources
Image 1 - gotboondoggle.blogspot.se
Image 8 - Source: Istockphoto
Image 9 - *Mattias Brodén*
Image 2, Image 10 – *WCM Consulting AB*
Image 24:24 - Intertechna AB

Other images: Oskar Olofsson

Cover – xsodia

Succeeding with 5S
© 2015, Oskar Olofsson
Published by WCM Consulting AB

ISBN: 978-91-637-4008-4

Contents

Introduction – the goal is a change of culture

With my work, I am often out traveling and visiting many different workplaces.

Throughout my visits, I often find traces of previous attempts to introduce the 5S method. Many times, the teams have worked hard, but sadly have not succeeded in creating long-term results.

Among those "traces" of the old attempt is a 5S file that no one looks at anymore, a tool board with no tools, or a few *before-and-after* pictures on another board.

I think that both the strength and the challenge of 5S is that the concept offers a way to change the culture of the company for the better. Sadly, this point is often forgotten in courses and books. 5S is presented as a relatively simple step that should be completed as fast as possible in order to move on with other kinds of improvement initiatives that are considered more profitable.

For that reason, in this book, I will describe ways to improve behavior and attitude concerning 5S to more successfully create long-term results with many direct and indirect positive effects. Instead of using common, but largely ineffective, methods to change attitudes, such as kick-off parties, advanced salary systems or leadership courses, we introduce tools that make all of us, each day, *act* better in our everyday work.

When these good habits are repeated, they represent the foundation of an improved company culture.

Should the least orderly be able to set the standard?

In many work places, people think that the housekeeping standard is already way too low – an opinion often shared by both managers and co-workers. Therefore, you might think that it shouldn't be very hard to make changes when almost everyone agrees that they're necessary.

However, there is a big problem that needs to be handled first. Everyone wants order, but no one wants to clean up after someone else.

Let's imagine that a workplace has just had a very important visit. Maybe the Swedish king popped in. While preparing for the visit, you cleaned for several days and everything was sparkling and fresh. After the visit, you said to each other: Imagine having our workplace this clean all the time!

Despite that sentiment, how long does it take before everything starts looking like it did before? A week? A month? Six months? Why don't we just maintain the order that was created when we know that that is what everyone wants? Most of us are rather neat and organized anyways.

I think the process of a clean and orderly workplace reverting back to a dirty one usually looks something like this: The first time a neat and orderly person comes to work and finds their workplace in an unclean or bad condition, perhaps he or she tidies up a bit and just thinks that the person who made the mess probably had a bad day.

Imagine that this happens a few more times, and the orderly person continues to tidy up and sigh a bit, but eventually, even the most orderly person will get tired of picking up the slack. Instead, the person thinks:

"No one else seems to care, why should I bother?"

Instead of cleaning everyone else's mess, they start to adjust and leave places dirty too. Slowly but surely, everyone begins accepting a standard that is below what they initially wanted to see.

What has happened is that they have unwillingly let the employee with the *lowest* standard for order set the standard for everyone.

Common standards

What separates 5S from your previous approaches is that we *jointly* decide a number of standards for how we want everything to be. These standards create and maintain the desired situation and become something to which we can compare the reality.

The first standard is how we want everything to look. This is often documented with pictures.

The second standard is how and when every 5S task should be performed, along with a visualization that makes them easy to remember.

The third standard is how every leader should act. The goal is to make it easier to be a good leader by investigating whether or not the system works, and also to standardize how the follow-up should be performed.

By working with these standards, we prove to ourselves and others that we care. When we see problems begin, we work in a structured way to permanently rectify those problems.

5S represents more than just order; it stimulates a change in the culture that will radically affect your workplace for the better.

Background – is this a new thing?

I think that people have always been aware of the fact that good order and cleanliness make it easier to perform good work of a high quality and maintain personal wellbeing. The problem has been about how to maintain that order.

Should we do it like in the military service, with daily check-ups of how stretched the sheets are and whether there is any dust on the windowsill? Or perhaps a simple request on a note in the kitchen that says, "Your mom does not work here, tidy up after yourself!" Or should we simply trust that we are all adults, and the problem will work itself out?

What separates the 5S method from other frequently failed attempts to improve order is that it consists of five logical and clear-cut steps that all depend on each other.

You could say that 5S creates order and maintains cleanliness in a systematic manner. The system is the most important component. In the initial three steps, we build the foundation for the two finishing steps, where we make sure that every day meets our desired standard.

Why was 5S developed in Japan?

The phrase 5S was coined by Hirano Hiroyuki, who described the method in the book *5 Pillars of the Visual Workplace.*

A clue to why it originated in Japan and not another country can be found in this picture:

Image 1: Japanese example

No, that is not a hired cleaner. The man in the picture is actually the CEO of a large corporation who has come down from his office to take part in the work. This enthusiasm for teamwork and unified responsibility, which can be found throughout the company, is one of the reasons why 5S has become a long lasting and important part of many Japanese companies' work methodology.

I think another reason why 5S was developed in Japan is the culture. I have taken the fast train in Japan a few times, also known as the Shinkansen. What struck me was that even though nearly all of the travelers were eating from a "bento box" during the trip, there was not a single crumb to be found on the floor (a bento box is a form of take-away food which often consists of rice or noodles and other vegetables or small side dishes).

I have learned that for Japanese citizens, it almost feels unnatural and wrong to leave your seat in a state that was not as clean as possible.

Shifting this view to the workplace was probably not a major step.

> Do you have to clean a bit extra before an important visit?
>
> Then you do not have 5S.

Is 5S simply a cleaning campaign?

All organizations have probably tried to improve their order and cleanliness. A lot of times, this takes the form of campaigns leading up to important events or visits.

I think that you should see 5S as the end of campaign cleanings.

I usually ask one important question when I visit a workplace and they tell me that they already work with 5S:

"What happens if a very important guest comes to visit?"

If the answer is that they would have to clean a bit more than usual, then they don't have a fully working 5S system yet.

They may have 5S boards, 5S hats, 5S posters or various 5S projects, but they have not succeeded in creating a real 5S culture.

In this guide, I will describe my own experiences in implementing this method.

I have educated over a hundred professional teams on 5S. In the beginning, I used the standard method from Japan. During the process, however, I have broken down the steps and made them a bit simpler, so that the idea will be easier for everyone to understand.

A milestone occurred when I let go of the rule that all of the steps should begin with the letter "S".." Instead, I started using simpler words. I noticed that the number of skeptics in the groups dropped dramatically!

The goal is to use 5S to create a real change of culture and also lay the foundation for even more improvement work, for example with Lean.

In this book, you will find four case studies from companies in completely different sectors that used 5S in a very successful way to achieve their goals.

You will read about how Trioplast halved all of their waste with 5S and other methods, and about how one major corporation used 5S in their journey to becoming a world-class producer.

As you will notice, 5S does not only work with production. One case study discusses how Holmen uses 5S to speed up the process of writing monthly reports and how Adrito uses 5S for handling documents.

What is common with all of these examples is that they have stubbornly remained dedicated to performing 5S, so that it is now an integrated part of the company culture.

Why 5S?

There are many different reasons for implementing 5S. You will achieve a number of direct gains, like improved safety, wellbeing and productivity, but also indirect gains, such as building the foundation for further improving the company. Let's start by exploring the direct gains.

Image 2: 5S requires cross-functional teamwork

5S for improved safety

One of the most important arguments for using 5S is that it will likely lower the risk of accidents. From the very beginning, this concept was developed to increase the safety level, and this is still a large part of its purpose.

Some have even wanted to put a bit of extra thought into the safety aspect, and have therefore added an extra S to the five S's - Safety and Health. However, others argue that safety is well integrated into the whole concept, making the extra "S" a bit unnecessary.

How is safety improved?

- No items are lying on the floor. This lowers the risk of falling over or getting caught in something, which could result in injury.

- The safety equipment is always in the right place and potential faults can be discovered more easily.

- Less dust and dirt helps to avoid the risk of slippery floors or dirty tools on which you can hurt yourself.

- Less of a mess gives you a clearer overview and lowers the risk of making poor decisions.

The important thing to remember is that safety is improved by being serious about keeping everything in order. When everyone starts following the routines and rules, a safe and secure circle is created.

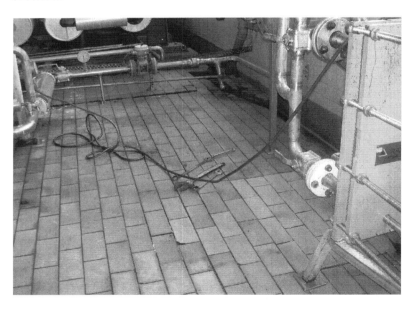

Image 3: Risk of falling over

5S for increased wellbeing

By creating a good working environment we get a workplace that we like better. Dirty, cluttered spaces that no one seems to care about don't help anyone. Working in a functional and clean place creates good feelings and pride.

Since 5S depends on you being a willing part of creating a better workplace through teamwork, the result of which will be something to be proud of. Motivation and morality increase when you have proven that you can personally make a difference and improve your establishment.

> Everyone should be able to work at a workplace that they can proudly present to others!

This increased motivation is a big reason why 5S is often the first step towards other concepts, such as Lean or World Class Manufacturing. When implemented correctly, 5S creates the habit of positive changes that are built on standardization, visualization, and more present leadership. This makes the next step towards more efficient work much easier.

Image 4: Teamwork increases motivation. Picture from a 5S Sorting inventory.

5S for the environment

Another important reason for implementing 5S is the risk of releasing waste into the oceans and the air if the workplace is messy. Perhaps a machine is leaking oil, or an air-suctioning cap is not working correctly. If we do not regularly clean or maintain things like this, it may take a long time to discover the problem, which can have serious consequences for the environment.

When things are in order, we may not need as much workspace as before. This will mean that we do not need as much heating or cooling, which is also better for the environment. The excess space and energy can be used for more important things, like producing new products that may make the company more profitable.

Image 5: Poor conditions or a lack of order mean environmental risks

Increased productivity and quality by making fewer mistakes

Every time we perform a task, there is a risk of making an error. The probability of mistakes is increased by factors like distraction, tiredness, misunderstanding, or stress.

One of the goals of 5S is to lower these risks. The main idea is that it should be easier to do something right than to do it wrong. Everything that disturbs the daily work process should be fixed.

To do a good job, we need appropriate and functioning tools, and a workplace where we are not always distressed by other things.

During the 5S implementation, we make sure that we have updated instructions at the right place to help with the work. Using pictures or a video as a complement to a written text makes it easier for everyone to understand how to work best.

It should be easy to do the right thing!

Another reason for many errors is the small but annoying faults in the equipment or bugs in the computer programs. More experienced workers may have grown used to them and found work-arounds, but they still affect the work flow, especially for newly hired staff.

Knowing and compensating for these minor flaws is sometimes mistakenly labeled as a skill, but the most skilled worker should not simply be the one who has learned all of the flaws in the establishment.

Instead, a skilled worker should be a person sharing their experience with others, participating in the standardization of work, educating others into their way of working, and proposing ways for improvement to upper management.

Increased productivity by less searching

During courses, I usually ask what aspect of 5S would make the most difference at your workplace. The answer that often comes up first is "no searching."

By having the right tools in the right place, the frustration of not being able to find what we need will disappear. That allows us to save time and avoid buying new equipment simply because we can't find something in the mess.

During the implementation phase, a common agreement is established on which tools one should have (and not) and where they should be placed.

Image 6: No more searching

Increased productivity by better reliability

Do you get a lot of "strange faults" from electronic systems? Faults that may come and go and are hard to investigate and do something about?

A lot of times, these problems exist because of dust or dirt in the air. By working with 5S, leakage is lowered and cleaning is done more often. This makes both the equipment and the staff work better!

By regular cleaning in the right way, there will be less dirt and wear on moving parts. This is very important for increasing reliability and giving clear results in automated production. (It may be important to point out that the wrong kind of cleaning may make the reliability worse, such as by using a pressure washer. Always read the manuals before introducing new cleaning routines!)

Another important reason why 5S improves equipment up-time is that when you clean properly, you will find faults. Maybe a cover is loose, or perhaps air tubes are leaking. By discovering faults early on, there is a possibility of doing something before it has grown into a full-on problem. This results in lower overall maintenance costs and more reliable production.

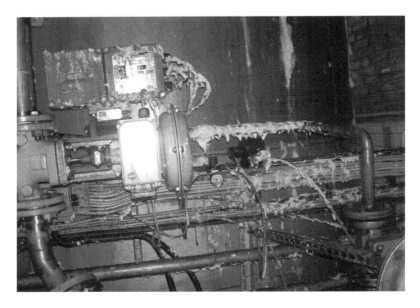

Image 7: Dirt creates "strange faults"

Cleaning as a part of 5S is, in many cases, the first step towards introducing increased operator participation in maintenance activities, called autonomous maintenance or TPM (Total Productive Maintenance).

Image 8: A good impression

Indirect gains with 5S

Working after a standard that is always being improved is a supporting pillar of successful concepts like Lean Manufacturing and Total Quality Management.

A strong argument for 5S is that it stimulates learning within the organization concerning why we should start working in a more standardized way, and what changes are necessary to get there.

What we will learn from 5S is that to successfully work towards a standard, we need to discover any deviations early, as well as analyze and initiate remedies. To achieve this, managers on all levels need to work more closely with their co-workers than before. An important goal in 5S is to simplify the job of being a good manager, since everyone after the 5S implementation knows what should be done and how. If there are deviations from the standard, then it will be easily spotted so that the root cause can be found. Working and improving the 5S System is therefore a good first step to becoming a "Lean Manager."

Another indirect reason for introducing 5S is that it creates more enthusiasm and a sense of responsibility among the employees. When everyone sees that it actually is possible to improve the situation with simple methods, future improvement to the working process will be much easier. Things that we have considered irritating for years will finally be rectified, and the frustration of not being able to find what you need will be eliminated.

When we are done, it will be very clear that improvements have occurred, and we know that the credit is largely due to our system. This creates enthusiasm and motivation, making 5S the first step towards all improvement work.

A better impression

Why are you skeptical about leaving your car in a dirty and unorganized workshop? Even if you know that their staff is professional and efficient?

It's easy to imagine that if the workshop cannot even handle being organized, then they may also have trouble handling the car. Will it get scratched? Can they really find all of the minor flaws? Are they going to keep track of the car keys?

The same concept applies to all workplaces. If we can keep every-thing in order, then a visitor will have an easier time believing that we are capable of performing our high-quality work. Later, you will read the case study from Aditro, where you will see how mak-ing a good impression makes it easier to get new customers.

Good order is obviously important when welcoming customers or other visitors. Something that is easily forgotten is how important it is to also make a good impression on guests from within the company. Decision makers are more inclined to risk money on investments or new products if the staff shows that they can take care of the establishment that is already in place.

This becomes especially clear in larger corporations with multiple production sites, but it also applies when you are deciding on whether or not to create a new product yourself or to pass it off to a subcontractor.

Case study – 5S for faster reports

Mattias Brodén is the business development manager at Holmen Paper AB. He has been responsible for implementing 5S in administrative processes, as well as around-the-clock production.

Holmen is a forest industry company that produces print paper, cardboard and wooden products; it has establishments within the forestry and energy industries and employs about 4000 workers.

OO: Can you describe how you worked with 5S in the administrative process?

MB: A statistics team worked to put together monthly statistics and reports. The team consisted of two people. It took three weeks to put together a report and the work created a lot of stress. For example, free days and vacations were often impossible at the end of the month.

         A downsizing of the organization made it possible for one of the people in the group to be offered early retirement. So there we were, with six weeks' worth of work and only one person to do it – an impossible situation.

         Since I had previous experience with 5S from the production environment, I thought that we should be able to use the 5S methods here as well. By investigating the purpose of every step in the process, I thought that it would be easy to transfer that way of working into this administrative process.

OO: In what way did you work with 5S?

MB: We started with the "Sorting Step" and tried to get rid of everything unnecessary and cut down on waste. We put together a list of all the work being done and asked the receivers of the reports if they really needed them to continue with their work. It turns out that only about 50% of the reports actually created value. The other half was simply wasteful and could easily be removed!

We then moved on to the "Set-in-order Step." This is where we organized all of the reports in the right order so that we would always do the most important first and the least important last. This decreased the stress of working with everything at the same time under pressure and also reduced the amount of waste in the process. The priority list became the first page in a numbered Table of Contents in a binder.

During the "Shiny Clean Step," we looked at what could be automatized. This showed that many of the lasting reports could be done automatically with a bit of coding and feeding the computer with fresh start and finish dates.

In the "Standardize Step," we made simple standardized instructions for each report. The goal was that anyone with limited training would be able to step in and replace the regular statistics staff. Every instruction was placed behind a numbered tab in the binder. In this way, the priority list/Table of Contents was connected to an instruction. For example, if you wanted to read about how to write the Economy report, just open Tab 1.

The last step was "Sustain." After each point in the Table of Contents, a row was added containing the months from January to December. When a report was finished at the end of every month, it was now easy to just check it off on the priority list. If the regular staff was ever sick, the sub could simply open the file and see how far along the process was, and then continue from there.

OO: How did that work out for you?

MB: The result was that we went from three weeks with a specialist to four days for a substitute. For the first time in seven years, the regular staff could now go on vacation by the end of a month, and I could even substitute for her myself!

OO: And now you work with 5S throughout the production site?

MB: Yes, that is correct. We are about halfway through the 5S implementation with 350 employees.

OO: Why did you choose 5S as a work method in production?

MB: The main reason was safety. Before implementing 5S, we had a lot of accidents, which were often simply caused by sloppiness. An example of this could be stumbling on hoses that were lying on the floor or tools lying where they could fall on someone's head. We needed order around the processes to create a normal level. The goal was that this standard would be safe, efficient, and would reduce the need for extra cleaning time before important visits.

In this way, we save time by making sure that everything is always in the right place. A lot of time used to be spent on searching for tools and materials, which did not add any value to the company.

OO: How did you implement 5S into the production process?

MB: We started with an introductory course for all of the managers and employees, which they took together. The purpose of this was to inform them about our goals and what was actually going to happen.

Thereafter, we divided the department into smaller areas and hired extra resources on the day during the implementation period. This replacement person would relieve the regular worker so they could participate in the 5S work. Every morning, we had a meeting with the production engineer to agree on what should be done. Every afternoon, a follow-up meeting took place.

In the first step, we put all of the items and materials in two piles. Those marked with red would be thrown out and those marked with yellow were things we had not decided on. The maintenance department and department leaders approved of everything before an item was thrown out. What remains is a working environment that only contains the materials that are needed and used within that area.

In the second step, we organized tools and materials based on how often and where they were used. Previously, there had been shift lockers, one locker with tools for each shift, but there was still always a mess and things often went missing. Now, we have boards put up with outlines of the tools that show where they are supposed to be. We have also drawn lines to show how much production material should be delivered to the production floor. Previously, the truck driver might bring out a week's worth of material in one day. All of the waste and chemicals in the area was also counted, and the amount of material needed between refills was estimated.

In the third step, we clean. The goal was to reach a level where we no longer had to perform any extra cleaning before important visits. When we were done, we took pictures and documented what we considered to be the right level. This became the new standard.

The goal of the fourth step was to make it easy to find out how everything should look and what routines to follow in order to uphold the standard in a certain area. Every area has a 5S-Order-board with five sections:

1. "This is our area" – A situation plan where our responsibilities were marked.

2. "This is how it should look" – Pictures of what the standard should be that are shot after the third 5S step.

3. "This is how we take care of our area" – A work schedule divided by shift and day of the week. The operators and the ones responsible suggest what should be done and how often.

4. "This is how we want to improve the area" – Suggestions are put up. Every week, the suggestions are taken into a section meeting and acted on according to the PDCA model.

5. "This is how we make sure that the routines are being followed" – Every shift makes a round at the beginning of their shift to find deviations from the standard, document them on the board, and remedy them so that they are not left when the next shift starts. A mentality is strived for where everything that is handed over to the next person is correct.

(See image 9)

The fifth step is about making sure that everything is working. The operators on the shifts do this three times every day and every morning by reporting the 5S status at the morning meeting. I also do an even more comprehensive audit of every area at the end of the year.

OO: What effects have you seen since the implementation?

MB: It is hard to say that all the gains are because of 5S, since a lot of different improvement work is going on at the same time. However, 5S combined with a standardized way of working for cleaning and maintaining equipment with daily visual check-ups has increased our efficiency by three percent. That means a lot of money in our business.

The operators are also very pleased and are advertising 5S when they meet operators from departments that have not tried it out yet.

We showed the production to our CEO, who came on a surprise visit. I showed the difference between areas with and without 5S implementation and explained that the main goal was to not have to do any extra cleaning when he visits. He responded very positively to that!

OO: You have chosen not to work through the managers very much in the organization. Why?

MB: The managers have so much to do, so they do not have time to deal with the practical implementation. Instead we work through the production engineers. They are often the next generation of managers and I think it is a good thing that they participate in the process from the beginning. The operators personally perform these daily check-ups and they control deviations from the standard at the very beginning of their shift. This creates a stable system that works even when the manager does not have time to spare.

The manager is part of one check-up every day, so they are still a big part of the work.

OO: What is your advice to others who also want to use 5S?

MB: Start with good communication and be clear about the purpose. Why are we doing this?

Work calmly and methodically. Check every step before you move along. If you work with big areas, it is good to divide them up into smaller parts.

The most important thing is that 5S should not be seen as something unusual. Eventually, it should be a part of your everyday life and working process.

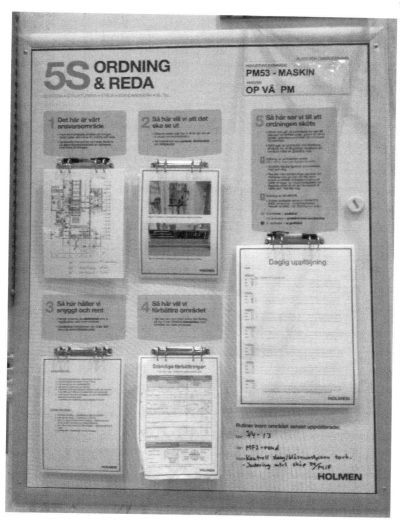

Image 9: 5S board at Holmen Paper AB. Text translation: 1. These are is our responsibilities 2. This is how it should look like 3. This is how we keep it clean 4. This is how we improve 5. This is how we follow up

The Five Steps

5S is built upon five Japanese words that all start with the letter S. Multiple attempts have been made to translate these into English "S-words", but I think that if you focus on that aspect, you risk losing sight of the main goal. I usually use these five following captions instead (with the traditional "S-words" in parentheses):

Sorting – In this step, you investigate and mark everything in the workplace that makes daily work harder, such as unnecessary things or non-functioning equipment.

Organizing (S-word: Systematic Arrangement or Set in Order) - Each item that you have agreed should be left should hereafter have a designated place based on how often it is used. Everything should be marked in a clear way. Workstations and workflows should be functional and have a good appearance.

Cleaning (S-word: Shine or Sweeping) – The work place is properly cleaned, based on a common standard that is agreed upon and the work to maintain that level is documented.

Routines (S-word: Standardize) – Routines are decided on and a system is introduced to see who will do what, making it clear whether the work has been done or not.

Discipline (S-word: Sustain) – The leadership gets help upholding the standard by introducing 5S audits on a schedule. Follow-ups and recognition ensure that the enthusiasm does not diminish.

Step One - Sorting

Sorting is the first step of 5S implementation. Here, we lay the groundwork for the following steps. If we are detailed with the Sorting Step, then the following steps will be much easier.

In this step we will sort things out, but that is not the only purpose of the Sorting Step. It is just as important to rectify known faults that make work unnecessarily difficult. Introducing new 5S routines will be hard if we have leaking pipes or are busy handling equipment that does not work as intended.

Sorting inventories

Sorting requires cross-functional teamwork that should be performed by all of the staff in the workplace.

At a production site, for example, both the production staff and the maintenance staff should work together so that two independent views of the matter can be formed. If you are working in shifts, you should encourage cooperation between the shift teams. Divide all of the employees into groups that make "sorting inventories" to find any of the unnecessary items and identify all the different kinds of waste.

Nothing should be placed directly on the floor or your workspace

Sorting out

We will start by looking at the first purpose – getting rid of unnecessary items.

What is an unnecessary item? Everything that is in the way or is making the cleaning process more difficult. The goal is to not have anything placed directly on the floor or on your work benches.

Remember that in a later step, we will make sure that everything is cleaned regularly. The fewer things we have lying around, the easier it will be to keep the space clean.

Go out in groups and examine each item critically. Then, discuss among yourselves:

Do we need this?

 - If not, recycle, give it away, or sell it.

Will we need it soon?

 - If not, place it in a storage room (for example, spare parts).

Some things may work, but still have other problems. Perhaps an item is hard to use, has a flawed design, or could affect the quality of the work.

In that case, it should be corrected or eliminated.

Every item that you think should be thrown out or fixed should be marked with a red tag.

The reason for marking items with a red tag is that it gives you an opportunity to react immediately to the suggested remedy. If it is obvious that it should be thrown out, then do so right away!

See image 10 for an example of a red tag.

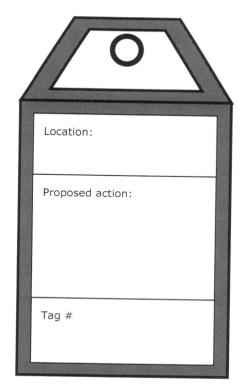

Image 10: Example of a red tag

What items should we look for to sort out?

How does it look behind or below the machines? Are there any outdated or unusable materials? Are there inappropriate things that you have grown used to over the years? It is easy to become blind to flaws that you are used to.

Are there any tools not being used? If so, why? Do we have tools that are worn down or broken?

Is there anything homemade, like something with tape and steel wire? This could indicate a need for tools, but homemade tools can also be impractical or dangerous.

Do we have broken spare parts in storage? Do we have excess spare parts? Are there spare parts for machines that are no longer running?

Do we have outdated instructions? What does it look like in binders or common folders in the computer system? Are there manuals in the right place and are old manuals cleared out?

Consider everything else that is not needed or is not in order. Old computer equipment? Packing material? Poor organization on the common network desks?

Sometimes, it can be hard to determine whether an item should be removed or not. Maybe you have a lot of "maybe-we'll-need-it" people in your organization that do not like to get rid of things.

If you are unsure, create a "quarantine area" where things can remain for a while before you make a decision or get rid of them.

The purpose is not to clear out things that you will need later on and have to buy again. The whole purpose of the Sorting Step is to work together and make wise and informed decisions.

Fixing known faults

During the sorting inventories we will also try to identify everything that is hindering us from working safely and efficiently. This is the second purpose of the Sorting Step – fix every known fault and come up with ideas for working towards improvement.

Here, we look at things like:

Outdated instructions

Is it possible to follow our instructions?

What we look at during the sorting inventories is mainly existing routines and instructions. Are they updated, valid, and being used? Are there notes put up with different kinds of instructions that could be collected and put in a more suitable place?

Within the borders of the 5S implementation, we will not be able to standardize everything. However, that is not what we want; instead we want every important task that directly affects the quality, reliability or safety to be performed the same by everyone.

Safety

Even if you have a working system for Health and Safety, you should also look at safety matters when you are doing the sorting inventories. The cross-functional way of working that involves everyone usually results in new suggestions being brought up.

What is needed to lower the risk of injuries or fires? Do we have the right standards in place on all electrical installations? Are there broken stairs, dangerous ladders, or other things creating risks around the workplace?

Environment

Is there anything we can do to lower the risk of environmental impact? Is it possible to discover possible leakage? Are sensors, alarms, and protection walls working?

Tools and equipment

Do we have the right equipment to do our work? Maybe the work would be easier if we had power tools, or is it possible to simply erase the need for certain tools with quick-release couplings or other methods?

Is anything missing? Is anything not working? Are there any suggestions for improvement?

Uncomfortable work

Are the seats and workspaces properly situated and are they easy to adjust? Are we being forced into bending, stretching, climbing ladders or heavy lifting? Are there bad physical work positions?

If we have uncomfortable or unnecessary tasks with repetitive steps, this needs to be rectified. It is hard to find time or be motivated to introduce new 5S routines if the workday is wasted on unnecessary physical labor.

Image 11: Uncomfortable work

Procrastinated maintenance

Do we have "permanent temporary solutions," namely emergency repairs with tape and steel-wire that have been done quickly to get production running again? Or are there other obvious technical faults, such as weird noises or smells, leakages, or loose parts?

Sometimes it is necessary to be creative, such as when trouble arises during a night shift. This can be fine (as long as all safety and quality aspects are considered). Maybe you will have to live with one small leakage from a machine and just put a bucket there for now, to be fixed as soon as possible.

One thing that cannot happen is for those temporary solutions or minor problems to become permanent. Small faults tend to grow and gradually risk creating chaos or increasingly less efficient work. Even these problems should therefore be investigated and fixed during the Sorting Step.

Suggestions for improvement

Are there ideas that may have been brought up earlier, but never put into action? Maybe the idea was pitched to someone who did not have time to look any further into it.

These ideas are also brought up during the Sorting Step, and then added to the same remedy list.

Documentation

Every item that is being removed and every discovered problem or suggestion for improvement is written on a red tag that is put as near to the problem as possible.

The red tags give a good visualization and create an increased motivation to get everything done.

The tags themselves are not enough though, since they easily fall off or disappear. That is why we also write down everything that we have written on the tags in an inventory list.

A red tag should not be up for more than 30 days

When you are done with the sorting inventories, you decide who is responsible for what and set due dates for each task. See image 11 for an example of how to visualize these action plans.

The tags should be taken down after 30 days. That should be the deadline for having completed the task or at least having made a plan for how you are going to handle it.

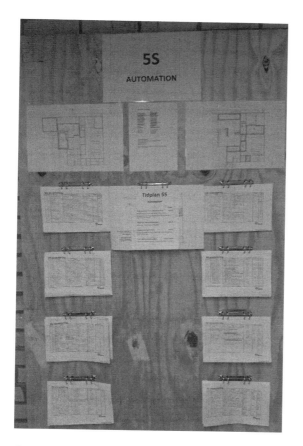

Image 11: Action plans after 5S sorting inventories

Alternatives to the red tags

Sometimes, it is not appropriate to place the red tags. For example, with grocery production, it is inappropriate to place a tag that may fall into the products.

An alternative is to place all loose items in two or three piles. Then, you can color code them with red for the things being thrown out, yellow for those things that should be fixed, and green for the things that should be put back in their proper place.

Sorting in an office

Sorting in an office environment is a lot like sorting in other spaces. Clean out everything unnecessary and rectify everything that makes the work unnecessarily hard.

A good way to think is that you should only have information in one place. Is it both digital and on printed paper? Is the information both in a central server and in your personal folders?

Another thing to question is whether you all have your own storage of office supplies, even though there is also a common one.

If several people share the office, you should, just like in all common spaces, cooperate during the sorting inventories.

If you work in individual offices, you should separate the places meant for common work tasks and personal work tasks. Therefore, you can agree on what should be the same for everyone and what parts should not be standardized and can vary with each individual.

The concept of "procrastinated maintenance" applies to computer systems as well. If the system is not regularly adjusted to a changing reality, it needs more and more manual work or workarounds to achieve a desired function.

Common traps during the Sorting Step

During the sorting inventories, you should try to get as many people as possible from the staff to join in, preferably at the same time. In that way, many decisions can be made directly, without needing to spend time with anchoring, repeating information, or explanations.

Include the maintenance, engineering, and environmental departments and managers directly so that you get as many perspectives as possible.

A common mistake is to write remedy lists, but then make someone who is not in the group responsible for the solutions. Many times, these solutions are forgotten. A good trick to avoid this is simply to not make someone from outside the group be responsible. You should retain the responsibility, whether you do the work yourself or get help from someone else. For example, talk to the right manager or write a work order for maintenance.

A risk with the Sorting Step in a production environment is that the maintenance department can be exhausted if you have a lot of procrastinated maintenance to take care of. One way to avoid this is to not start with all areas at the same time. Maybe wait a month between the start of different workplaces so resources aren't depleted or exhausted.

If the maintenance staff has been there for the whole sorting inventory, motivation usually improves by finding creative ways to solve the problems.

Also, consider the risk of being blind to certain flaws you are used to. One experienced person should walk around between the groups to check work and point to different things that the groups might have missed.

Case study - Losses cut in half with simple methods

Cornel Oancea is a Lean coordinator at Trioplast. He has worked with implementing Lean methods into factories in Smålandsstenar and has also worked with 5S at a factory in Saudi Arabia. Trioplast is a Swedish industry company with 1,300 employees.

OO: Why did you choose to work with 5S?

CO: We started with a kind of pilot in 2001 in the conversion department, of which I was then the boss. The project was called the "8-step Rocket." The first five steps of the rocket were 5S. The last three steps were operator autonomous maintenance. The pilot project succeeded, but sadly did not spread outside of the department.

In 2008, 5S first became a company initiative connected to a venture to raise profits leading up to a possible sale. An audit was done throughout the company and afterwards, the leaders from the divisions met.

A goal was set to cut manufacturing waste in half and we agreed on three areas to focus on: Common goals and key performance indicators broken down to every work team, 5S, and Visual tracking.

OO: How was the practical 5S work performed?

CO: We started by closing down one department at a time and clearing out all items. The items were put into three piles. The green pile was to be put back in place, the yellow pile consisted of things that needed rectifying, and the red pile was going to be thrown out or recycled.

The next step was to organize and label the items. Here, the first need for a common standard arose. We came up with a color-coding system for the floor markings and agreed on what width the tape we used should be.

Afterwards, we cleaned thoroughly. We closed one line at a time and cleaned everything thoroughly. The goal

was to get the equipment looking brand new. We re-
painted when needed. Then, we put a list next to the
machine and noted what became dirty in 24 hours and
where the dirt came from. Based on the list, we identi-
fied what needed to be fixed, what should be cleaned
regularly, and how often.

Then, we made instructions for the cleaning routines,
which we placed in the same place that the work was
to be done. Here, another need for standards arose. We
produced a template for these forms so that they would
look the same everywhere.

To make sure not to forget tasks, we brought out a visual calendar with dots that showed when different
things needed to be done. The calendar is also connected to a checklist.

OO: What do you do to maintain the standard?

CO: The production manager is responsible for making
        sure that everything is working. We also schedule reg-
        ular meetings where we investigate how things are
        going.

        On the internal computer network, there is a graph
        that shows how well 5S works in different departments
        right now. Based on an audit template, every depart-
        ment is also graded each month. If the score decreases,
        the production manager will have to explain himself.

OO: How did you get all of the managers interested?

CO: We implemented something that we called the TPS academy. We educated everyone in 5S and other methods so that they all knew what the big fuss was about.

It is important that all the managers on all levels are engaged in this and mean what they say. They also have to understand that it will cost money; you have to risk something in order to gain even more.

OO: What effects have you seen after implementing 5S?

CO: 5S has represented an incredible boost for us. Our goal was to cut manufacturing waste by 50% and we have achieved exactly that. In a factory like ours, everything has to be clean and the machines have to be top notch. Otherwise, we will get complaints or wasted resources.

One clear effect is that our owner did not complete the sale since the company is far more profitable now!

OO: Now that you have succeeded with 5S – what are you working on at the moment?

CO: It differs between factories, since we have different pre-conditions. In Jönköping, they work a lot with the SMED method to reduce setup times. In our factory, we are working towards making continuous improvements through root cause analysis work.

OO: If you had to give advice to someone else trying to succeed with 5S, what would you say?

CO: If I had that job, I would start by getting a clear view of how the establishment is actually working today.

I would then schedule a meeting with the managers and ask them to describe their biggest sources of man-ufacturing waste. Afterwards, I would ask them if they would like to cut that waste in half with simple meth-ods, and if so, whether they are prepared to do what needs to be done.

If they tell me that they are willing to do what is neces-sary, I would make sure to get it in writing before the work started!

Step Two – Organizing

When the Sorting step is finished, everything unnecessary will have been cleaned out, all leakages and sources of dust have been fixed and everything else disturbing daily work has been rectified.

Now, we must move on and work to find appropriate placement for everything that we chose to keep. This includes not just tools or other loose items, but the whole layout, including placement of the staff member workplaces, equipment, appliances and instructions. The goal is to create a flow as free from disturbance as possible and a visually clear workplace where we can easily get an overview and discover deviations from the normal.

Flows and visualization

The first thing that we should do is check if we have a suitable layout that provides an overview and simple workflows.

One way to analyze the current layout is to draw a "spaghetti diagram." You can see an example of this below. It can be used for material flows, document flows, or human movement. Map out the current situation. How are we actually moving about our work day and is this the optimal way of working?

With the diagram in hand, it will be easier to see the areas that need improvement.

If you see a need for change, map out a new layout that better matches with how you want to work.

It is hard to think of everything at once. Many times, multiple attempts are needed before you find the best solution. Begin with a temporary solution. This makes it easier for testing and moving around until you are happy.

To visualize how everything should be, we identify and mark different areas in the layout. That way, it will be easier to see if anything is in the wrong place and people who are not used to being on your premises will have a better understanding of how to move around.

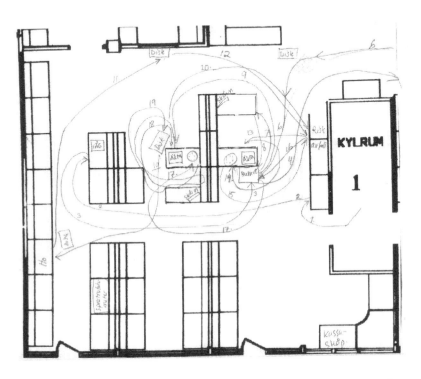

Image 12: Spaghetti diagrams make the areas of improvement clearer

Where does the material get in and out? How does it move around the establishment? Make it simple for everyone transporting material so that they clearly understand where it should be put down and picked up.

You should separate work surfaces, safety zones, storage space, machine surfaces and transport surfaces. Also, consider the ergonomics of every process. You should not have to repetitively bend your back or perform heavy lifting to pick up or move material.

Agree on a standardized color-coding system. A good piece of advice is to begin using tape that can be removed and changed. Do not paint the color-coding system permanently until you are sure that everything works.

Image 13: Use a color-coding system and mark the floor

Go over the storage space and mark maximum and minimum levels for inventory. This could be the beginning of a "Kanbansystem," where refilling is done when the storage levels have fallen beneath a certain level, instead of the material being delivered based on prognosis or other arbitrary reasons from the transporter.

Image 14: Visual storage

Tools and appliances

When we have the right layout, we can make sure that all tools and other items are in the right place.

Agree on where everything should be, then mark those spots and place the relevant items on the marked spots.

One rule is that it should only take a second to check that everything we need is there. A good example is shadow boards for tools. See image 15.

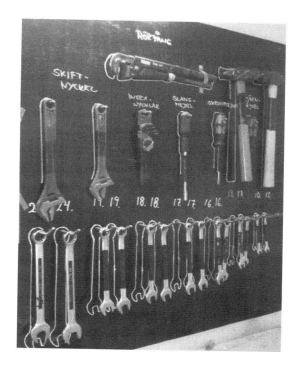

Image 15: Shadow board for tools

If possible, the tools should be placed exactly where they are going to be used.

The mindset is the same as arranging your kitchen at home. Plates that you use every day should be easy to access, but a holiday stew-pot that may be used once a year can be placed on the top shelf.

The best thing, of course, would be if we did not need tools at all. With the help of quick-release couplers and other solutions, the number of bolts and nuts may decrease. Standardizing the dimensions of bolts and nuts also ensures that as few tools as possible are needed. A good set rule is that you should only need three tools to get through your daily work as an operator.

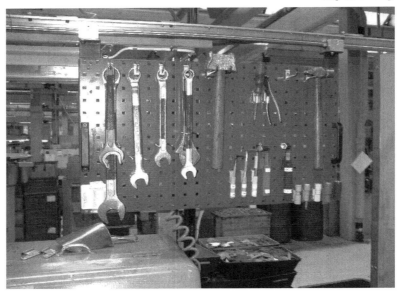

Image 16: A color-coding system shows where the tools should be used

Do you have tool boards, but they are missing tools?

In work places where the staff has grown used to the lack of tools, there is a risk of everyone creating their own little tool storage space. This makes the tool situation even worse, because it means you may keep the tools you get your hands on instead of putting them back where they belong.

To break this behavior pattern, you need to make someone re-sponsible for the tool board and make sure that it is checked on a regular schedule.

The best thing would be for the responsible person to find and restore all of the missing tools. However, if they are not found, you still have to refill the board with new tools, and repeat this until everyone is used to always having the tools in the right place, ra-ther than needing to collect their personal tools.

This is when the problem will finally disappear.

Office or administrative processes

The Organizing Step is also very important in administrative pro-cesses. It is about creating efficient workflows and new possibilities to help each other.

In personal offices, you need to standardize certain things that should be the same for everyone. This could be things like:

- Places for new and ongoing duties and ways to archive fin-ished ones.

- What sorts of files should be stored locally in the room and what should be in the common spaces?

- Which office supplies should everyone have and what should be in the common spaces?

The level of standardization depends on factors such as whether or not you have shared offices, the need to find materials in each other's offices, if you are working in the same process, or if every-one has their own work.

For example, you should not force everyone to mark where the pen should be in their personal offices; that is best decided by the person who works in the office.

At a workbench, however, which is shared by many people, it can be very important to mark the place for a pen. Why waste time searching for a pen just because everyone puts it away in different places?

A great deal of time can be lost in printer rooms or in rooms for common documentation. Agree on what the order should be and how different materials should be refilled. Mark appropriate places and refill levels and write clear instructions for things like error reports or maintenance.

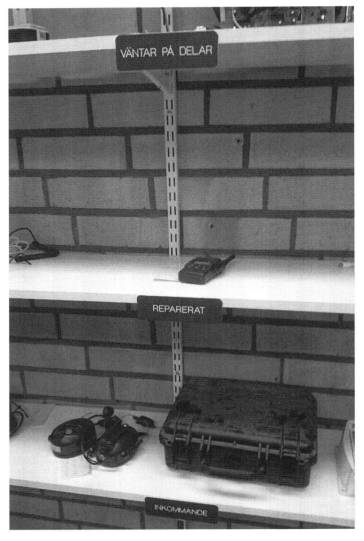

*Image 17: Prioritize standardizing things that simplify flow and coopera-
tion. Text translation: Incoming / Repaired / Waiting for spare parts*

With administrative processes, the flows are often not as clear as
with production. Here, the process could need visualizing on a
board where you can easily get an overview of where every task is

and if there is a problem somewhere. In that way, you can even out the workload and shorten lead times. During the Organizing Step, you can agree on how this board should look, where it should be placed, and how often you should meet by the board.

The easiest level is where every employee has their own "Kanban board," which provides an overview of all work duties. This will make it easier to do the most important tasks first. The board also helps you focus on one task at a time. It also signals both overload and free time, so that others know when to ask for favors and when to stay away. See image 18 for an example of a simple personal Kanban system.

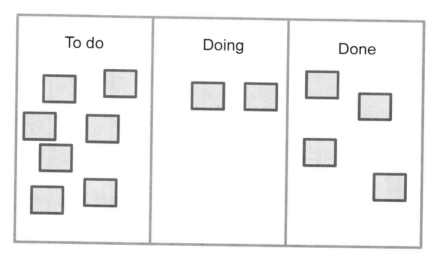

Image 18: Example of a simple personal "Kanban" system to visualize workload and problems

During the Organizing Step in administrative processes, you should improve the order and structure of the common networks. By agreeing on a good and logical file structure and rules for naming documents, it will become easier for everyone to find what they are looking for.

Common traps – the Organizing Step should not take up too much time!

The overall goal of the Organizing Step is to create "the perfect work flow." Unfortunately, it's easy to overdo it and start big projects that take up too much time. For example, investing in redesigning layouts or searching for advanced visual boards. Before all of these projects are done, the organization will have forgotten about the 5S system that you were working with in the first place, and the process will have to start from the beginning.

I recommend thinking of perfection as a vision, not as a qualification for moving on with the work.

Set a reasonably ambitious level and a time limit for the Organizing Step. Otherwise, you risk getting stuck and negatively impacting your work efficiency.

It is better to only include things that you are able to do within the time limit, such as simple layout changes, rectifying obvious problems, and implementing simple boards of the *"post-it on notepad"* variety. Leave the "perfecting process" for the improvement work, which starts with the audits in Step 5.

Storage space for special materials

A question that sometimes comes up during the Organizing Step is where to put special materials, such as products that are going to be corrected or things that you can't sell right now. Should they be close to the production area where there really isn't space, or should they be placed in a special storage space outside of the production establishment?

My advice for you is to not put away this material.

The reason that we have such a high inventory of these things is that there is a problem in production related to quality, planning, or something else. If we just put this problematic item away, we easily forget the problem, which increases the risk of us not dealing with the root causes.

Only reserve storage space for normal production and material. Special materials that are abnormal somehow should therefore be discovered easily and the cause should be dealt with.

Image 20: Well organised material

Step Three – Cleaning

The third step of 5S is to perform a thorough cleaning. I usually call this step the initial cleanse to point out that this is a one-time thing. In the future, we will create routines that will ensure that we keep to the new standard.

A lot of people call the third step "Sweep," but I think that is mis-leading, since that title often shifts focus to sweeping floors or dusting. The initial cleanse is a lot more intensive; it is meant to restore the equipment and establishment to looking almost brand new.

Image 19: Initial cleanse - clean inwards and outwards

During the Cleaning Step, we make everything as clean and spot-less as possible, which makes it a lot easier to later uphold the new standard. Along with the (temporary) gain of everything being clean and looking good, the initial cleanse has two other even more important purposes:

Firstly, we will establish a commonly decided standard of cleanliness – this is what we want it to look like after we clean! Documentation with pictures should be put up by the workspace.

Secondly, we will gain knowledge of how the facilities should be cleaned. This is documented and the documentation is used to create appropriate routines.

The difference between this and a regular cleaning is that we document the work

The people who have just cleaned a specific area become the specialists who can determine how often this should be done in the future and how long it will take each time, if we do it regularly.

Performing an initial cleanse

An initial cleanse is performed as an extra work task. If possible, close the production area entirely and clean during work hours. If not, then you will have to do the cleaning outside of normal working hours.

To perform the initial cleanse, you should divide the facility into smaller parts and work in teams, possibly in pairs.

Every team cleans (and simultaneously inspects) their assigned area. Remember that the goal of the cleaning is to restore the equipment and workplace to looking brand new.

Case study – Is it possible to stop production for a whole day?

A subcontractor within the automobile industry was recently performing an initial cleaning. This was quite difficult, since they delivered every day and had to be very flexible with the customers.

Therefore, they gave the customer an advanced notice about how the production would stop for one day due to 5S work. They were a bit worried about how the customer would react.

Instead, the answer they got was, "Great, you should have done that a long time ago! Just tell us when so that we are prepared."

What separates this cleaning from other cleaning you may have done earlier is that with this system, you document the work. Let every team register every place where they have cleaned:

- Where have we worked?

- What should be done *regularly* at this station?

- How *often* should it be done?

- Can we simplify future cleaning with better appliances, painted surfaces, or improved access?

- Lastly, the team will estimate how long the work would take if you performed it on a regular basis in the future.

What took two hours this time may only take a minute if done every week.

Afterwards, a team member takes a picture of the finished result to document the new standard. This is what it should look like after a cleaning!

Remember that this is a one-time "deep clean." During the next step, we create routines to uphold the new standard.

Investigating how the dirt comes back

In an industry environment, it can be good to complement the subjective judgment of how different cleanings should be done with a more objective investigation. This can be done by studying how quickly things get dirty again following an initial cleanse.

Appoint people who get an overview each day or each shift and document where the workspace gets dirty again and the source of the dirt. Then, try to get rid of all of the waste points.

If you are not able to get rid of the dirt coming in, you need to adjust the frequency of the cleaning routines so that the right cleaning standard is maintained.

Cleaning in an office environment

In an office environment, where you have your own personal office, it is natural that everyone cleans their own room. Then, you clean the common spaces together. If you have a shared office, you clean together and then agree on the new standard.

In an office, you should also add things like clearing out the mail inbox and whiteboard to the list.

Document everything you do, as this creates the foundation for your new routines. Also, do not forget to take pictures of the new standard.

Image 20: initial cleanse in an office environment

Agree on a standard

A standard is a common agreement on what condition we think is right for a certain place. Often, this standard is documented with pictures that are then strategically posted near the place depicted in the pictures.

The standard is used by everyone responsible for 5S routines in a workplace. By looking at the standard, you are reminded of how it should look after you have cleaned. By having a standard that has been commonly agreed on (provided that everyone partici- it to.

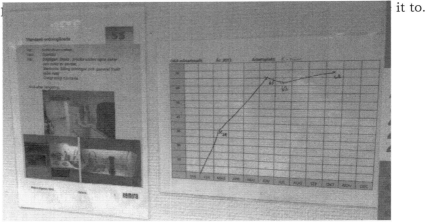

Image 21: Standard with pictures and monthly checkups

After a cleaning, if we have not obtained the same level as the agreed upon standard, that means we have a deviation.

The deviation is taken care of by team leaders or managers, and also represents an input for deciding on future improvement work.

Factors to consider when deciding on a common standard

Reliability and safety – How clean does the equipment have to be to avoid breakdowns, wear, or injuries?

Wellbeing – What is needed for us to feel good and proud of our workplace?

Quality – What level of cleanliness is necessary for our products to turn out at a high standard?

A good impression – How clean should it be for visitors to think the space looks good?

Is a reminder enough? Do we need to change the routine, educate more, permit more free time, or take an active decision to change the standard?

The result of a well-executed initial cleanse

An initial cleanse is a very important step in the 5S process. Doing it right will have the following effects:

- Everything looks clean and nice. "There is a whole new smell to the factory now!" is a typical comment.

- The workplace is easier to keep clean. Places with in-grained dirt are cleaned and improvements are made so that cleaning can be easier in the future.

- A first draft for cleaning routines that are well established, since everyone has participated in creating them.

- A sense of being on the right path – "Now we just have to make everything work!"

- Pictures function as the new standard. "This is what it should look like after cleaning."

Step Four – Routines

Now, we have a workplace where everything unnecessary has been cleared out, good flows have been created, there is a suitable place for everything, and the facilities are sparkling clean. Are we finished with 5S?

No, we're not, but unfortunately, too many 5S initiatives stop here – after only the third "S." What remains, however, are the two most important steps. The fourth step is where the culture begins to change for the better, in order to maintain the result.

The next step involves introducing working routines. 5S routines are produced to ensure that the new standard is upheld.

The documentation from the initial cleanse provides us with a good first draft for the new routines in which all of the employees have participated in making. Take this suggestion as a "best guess." The most important thing is to start following the routines so that you can begin improving upon them. Eventually, we learn about what is actually necessary and we perfect the way of working even more.

In some cases, the new cleaning routines should be examined by process owners and by maintenance staff, particularly when there is a risk of compromising the products by cleaning in a way that affects reliability. Also, all safety hazards need to be examined and handled appropriately.

Before we begin implementing new routines, we should consider whether it is possible to avoid the root problems causing the need for certain tasks. As part of the Sorting in Step 1, we have hopefully fixed the major causes for leakage or dust, or have found them as part of the Cleaning Step.

If anything remains, we should rectify that as soon as possible. The alternative is having a routine that includes cleaning the same place maybe once an hour, but that is normally not how we want to use our working hours.

Daily routines

Cleaning should be a part of the daily work *for everyone.*

This means that at least five minutes of every day should be spent cleaning your workplace. At a mechanical workshop, that would mean brushing away the chippings and removing waste. If you work in an office, you could end the day by putting away your work and sorting your loose files and documents.

Keeping your workplace clean should be seen as part of your work skills. Even if your work is good in other aspects, it is not appropriate to create a mess that may affect others or make it harder for you to find your things.

The daily routines should be written in the job description and instructions so that they become part of the daily work. Training is done when you are introduced to a new part of this work. It is important for it to be possible to follow up the daily routines. Therefore, the work duties should be reported in a visual checklist or some other simple system.

Image 22: Daily routines

Weekly routines

Some routines need to be done weekly. Many times, it is easiest to perform these tasks during a weekly cleanup. This is performed at a set time, if possible, or planned for a time when it causes the least possible disturbance.

Instructions for the weekly cleaning are put together in a 5S file or in some other suitable place.

Connected to the instructions there should be a checklist, which can be signed so that nothing is missed.

Do not forget to appoint someone to be responsible for updating the checklist and the instructions so that they improve and adapt to changes in the workplace over time.

What do you do when the weekly routines cannot be done? Maybe there were two trucks waiting to be loaded when you scheduled your cleaning. In this case, you cannot just skip your 5S duties. You have to do two things: Find a corrective action – possibly scheduling them for the following Monday morning —and try to improve your planning so that these problems do not arise again.

Unusual tasks

Some tasks should be done less often, such as every two weeks, every month, or even less frequently. These kinds of tasks are the hardest to maintain as a part of the routine, since they are hard to remember. You need some kind of system that reminds you what should be done and who is responsible.

Let's consider the task of opening a locker and cleaning the inside. It's not necessary to do this every week, but maybe every two months. How are you going to remember to do this and the person responsible for the work?

You need some form of working order system to help. The system needs to tell you what should be done, who is responsible, and when it was last finished.

What system fits your organization the best is up to you, but it needs to be visual for everyone and easy to follow up on.

Planning arrays

One possible way is to create big arrays in, for example, Excel, to show who should do what and when.

"Work task" and "Responsible person" are written into the row headlines and "Execution week" should be in the columns. Then, you color code the chart to show when every task should be done.

If you print it out on a large enough piece of paper, everyone can sign directly into the array when they are done with a task.

This can be a working system as long as you do not have too many duties. The problem arises when you want to update or increase the number of tasks. Then, you have to print out a new array, which eliminates the historical documentation.

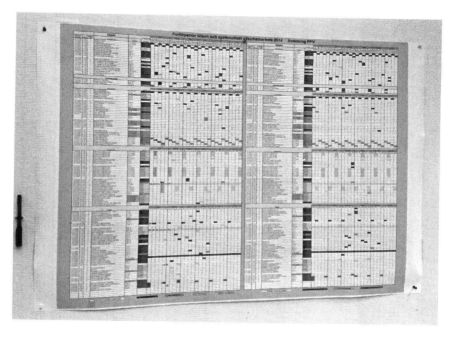

Image 23. Planning array

Computerized systems

Some organizations with a computerized maintenance system use it for 5S routines. The presumption for this to work is that everyone uses the maintenance system regularly, which is seldom the case. Often, the maintenance system is only used on a daily basis by the maintenance staff.

By using handheld equipment, you can establish a working system that is used by everyone. The positive of this is that the handheld unit allows you to add instructions in the form of pictures or a video to simplify the work and to make it possible to report any deviations immediately.

These kinds of handheld systems are most common in bigger establishments, where the demands of traceability and history of operation and maintenance are vital, such as in nuclear plants. The reason is that implementing the system is very time-intensive work and costs quite a bit; it is therefore not that profitable for smaller facilities.

Image 24: Example of a handheld computerized system

Planning boards

In many cases, visual manual planning boards are the best option. They provide a quick overview, are accessible to everyone, and easy to understand. The style of these boards varies with each establishment.

The principle is that you produce 5S cards with one green side and one of another color – let's say blue (the color red is common, but should be reserved for deviations). On the cards, you write what should be done and where. You can refer to instructions if necessary. Then, sort the cards by how often the routine should be done, such as weekly, monthly, or quarterly. Then, take out a board with one column for every pile of cards and place them in an easily visible place with the blue side facing out.

Every routine that should be done weekly is placed in one column, monthly in another, and so on.

When a routine is performed, you simply turn the card over. Every Monday morning, the team leaders or another designated person turns all of the weekly cards back over. At the beginning of each new month, the monthly cards are turned over. Se image 25 for an example.

This system is easy, highly visual, and works well in many facilities. Staff that work in shifts could also use the boards to know which shift team is responsible for what duty.

Image 25: Simple planning board with weekly, monthly and quarterly duties

If you have a complicated establishment with many shifts and personnel moving throughout large areas (for example, in the process industry), then the best solution is usually a big planning array with 5S cards. (See image 26). Here, you can see every column on the board represents a week and every row represents a shift team. Include enough columns so that the planning covers at least a quarter of a year. The cards are then placed on the planning board. Normally, you give the assignment to the shift team that can perform the task at a suitable time. When the task is done, the card is turned over.

This means that, for example, one shift team is responsible for five duties every week. No task should take longer when considering this normal reliability and familiarity.

When the weeks are over, the cards are turned back.

Image 26: Planning board with 5S cards. Process industry with shifts.

No matter what system you choose, you need to appoint someone to be responsible for maintaining and updating the system.

Common Traps during the Routine Step

A common mistake is distributing personal responsibilities within all fields i.e., Steve is responsible for this area, Ann is responsible for that area, and so on. Even if that level of personal responsibility does work for a while, there is inherent instability in this system.

If someone is home sick or leaves the group, there is a risk that the system will stop working. There is also a risk that people will start thinking, "I've done my part, I don't need to worry if something looks bad somewhere else," rather than helping when someone is having trouble keeping up.

A better choice is to give a more general responsibility to a smaller group or shift team. When needed, a team leader regularly distributes the groups' duties. If you are a mature team, however, you can take care of this yourself.

Case study – Begin with the manager's office

Anna-Carin Söderlund works as a WCM Champion at a major international company and has led the implementation of 5S at several factories.

OO: When did you first come in contact with the 5S method?

AC S: The first time was in 2002, when I worked as a Lean Manager at a big industrial company in the vehicle industry. I was appointed to implement 5S at a facility with 650 people. It required major effort that included everyone: production, offices and workshops. We worked broadly and took it one step a time across the whole factory. We used leadership seminars, co-worker seminars, brought out education materials, created websites, and worked a lot with coaching.

We started with 90 work teams at once. It was very hard, and today, I would probably not work as broadly as that, but we just started and solved problems when they came along. The benefit of working at the same time was that all the managers could cooperate, learn from each other, and share experiences.

OO: How do you work with 5S at your current work-place?

AC S: Where I work today, we implement 5S more from need. We are clear about why we are going to make the change and what the goal is. This sometimes means that we cannot simply pick 5S as our first tool; sometimes, it can be used to reduce setup time or operator maintenance, but the 5S way of thinking has to be maintained all the same.

In the beginning, we always offer a course for the employees where we go through the whole concept and give some examples. We take the team that is going to work with 5S to an area where it has already been implemented in order to demonstrate good examples and discuss experiences.

It's important to never leave the project group without support or coaching. It can be easy for me or someone who is competent and knows the work method, but this is a new concept for many people.

We perform an audit after every step, and we have to agree on appropriate levels. It is easy to accidentally set the standard too low, but I want there to be a common standard throughout the factory.

OO: Why do you think working with 5S is important?

AC S: To me, 5S is the foundation. It trains people and teams to work structurally and follow a standard. At the same time, managers are trained through follow-ups and actually learn to do what they say they are going to do.

The gains with 5S are extensive. Safety, healthy working environment, environmental protection, quality control, efficiency, and reduced costs are just a few examples. The direct gains we see from 5S represent a risk reduction, which we measure by fewer risk points.

The indirect gain of 5S is much bigger than often believed, because it creates a change of attitude and culture. If you start thinking in an organized, responsible, and dedicated way, it spreads into other areas.

An important argument for us is the impact it has on visitors. In what way do important clients view our production?

OO: What is important to think about when implementing 5S?

AC S: It is important that you get the managers engaged. They have to act as role models and understand what 5S really means. We usually start with their offices. If they cannot get their own office in order, then it is hard to demand that others change their behavior. This is true even for the highest manager.

Another thing that must be considered is to not try to include everything with 5S. Do not try to solve every problem there is with these methods. If you do that, you run the risk of not making any progress in a timely manner. Always use the right tools for the appropriate problems.

Make sure you have working plans for follow-ups, both by your own team and from the management.

OO: If you were going to give advice to someone thinking of working with 5S, what would it be?

AC S: Start with visiting someone who has already succeeded. Watch and learn and try not to set your bar too low.

Express yourself like a leader. You have to be able to answer the question, *Why am I doing this?* Otherwise, it will easily become an ordinary cleaning project. Start with your office to learn and then show others the right way.

Then, you simply start and solve the problems as they come along. A smart thing to do is to start with one area and do a really good job on it. Then, you have an example to show others.

Remember that, as a manager, you have to follow up. One way to do this is to schedule a follow-up every Friday to see what has been done and make sure that the work is going in the right direction. Follow-ups should take a coaching approach. Do they need support?

You have to show that you are serious and that you are also working within the same system.

Step Five – Discipline

Now, it's finally time to finish off the work. It is not enough to have the best routines in the world – you also have to follow them...

To make 5S viable, we have to repeat our routines until they are a natural part of our work process. The best thing is if it becomes a habit without you having to think about it.

Compare it to learning to brush your teeth. As a kid, you would protest every morning and night when it was time. After a while, you learned to accept it and would eventually brush your teeth twice a day without thinking about it. As an adult, you are so used to the feeling of clean teeth that it would feel weird to leave the house without it.

Making the routines work does not just mean telling everyone that it is their responsibility to follow them, not even if you all agree that it is the right way to go.

> The manage-ment has the responsibility to follow up on the routines

It does not help to put up instructions on a pin board or discuss them in meetings. I think the problem lies in our human nature to perform passive resistance. Sooner or later, you will try out *not* following the routine. If no one cares, then you will begin to think that maybe the rule was not so important after all.

The responsibilty for getting the routines to work, following up, and keeping the system running lies with the managers and leaders. The goal of Step Five – Discipline is to help the managers do a good job by introducing efficient tools:

Audits

A very efficient way to maintain 5S is to schedule regular audits.

The purpose is to get the managers to take responsibility for maintaining the routines and show that they are still serious about 5S. By using a coaching attitude, the audit team will discuss problems with the staff and help everyone to find solutions.

Decide on a schedule and assign who is to participate at different times. By adding the audits to the calendar, you ensure that they are not forgotten.

The audit schedule should have several levels.

Example:

Each day

- The oncoming shift performs a control sweep to make sure the workplace is left in the correct state. Deviations are noted and discussed with the closest manager.

Each week

- Self-monitoring by the work team or by a team leader at their own workplace. Have all the routines been executed according to the plan? If not, is there something we can fix ourselves? Do any routines need changing? Hand in any suggestions you have for changes.

Each month

- Managers ensure that the self-monitoring is working and perform a sweep, setting points according to a pre-decided template (see the example in Appendix 1.) The points are placed visibly for everyone to access.

Every three months

- Higher management performs an audit to check that 5S is working as planned and discusses how to improve the system with leaders.

Each year

- A reconciliation of the past year. Is the workplace still in the intended state? What have we learned from this?

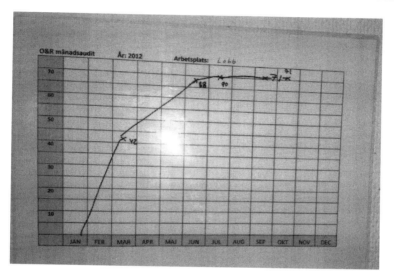

Image 27: *Points from the monthly checkup*

When it is time to agree on the frequency of the audits, it is good to consider how big of a culture change 5S will represent. In a case where 5S means a big change, I recommend that the management participate in the follow-up rounds more often, perhaps every week, until the routines work. When everything is stable, you can transition to monthly audits.

Diplomas and other rewards

An important part of succeeding with 5S is to celebrate success.

One way is to implement a reward system where different parts of the facility get a diploma when they have proven that they can maintain 5S for a certain period of time.

Image 28: *Visualization board that provides an overview of 5S initiatives*

A nice diploma can be encouraging for the work team. You may add a sticker for every year, to show that the workplace continues to meet the established standards.

The big picture should be visualized on a board where the progress of 5S for every department is clear, and areas that have received diplomas have a special marker.

In connection to the diplomas, you might want to reward the group somehow, maybe with a cake or a group dinner. When every group has a diploma, it might be fun to do something together to celebrate the group's success.

I do not think that you should associate 5S with any economic bonus, either individually or for the whole team. The reason is that economic perks risk creating jealousy or expectations that 5S should only be performed if extra pay is earned. This means that your goal of making 5S a natural part of the work becomes harder, and the way of working will be seen as something special, not as natural common sense.

Tie 5S together with a quality management system

To get the 5S routines to become part of your regular management, 5S should relate to the way of working in your ordinary quality management system (such as 9001 and others). The connection is easily made with the expression "we work with order and cleanliness in the following way..." The details, such as check lists, 5S cards, etc. should normally not be written into the quality management system. There need to be changes often and locally by the individual staff.

In cases where cleaning is a legislated part of the quality system, such as in the food or pharmaceutical industry, you can divide cleaning into the type that affects quality and the type that does not.

For example, an ordinary quality system with its traceability and version control can be used to run the cleaning of production that affects parts of the equipment, as well as an easier system, such as one in which 5S cards can be used for less sensitive cleaning of the facility.

Other ways to maintain 5S

Some companies consciously put pressure on themselves by regularly inviting customers and important clients to visit. That way, you can show the progress you have made and reduce the risk of losing your focus.

Another way to increase motivation and pride for the workplace is to arrange family days. Maybe you can show your family before-and-after pictures and tell them more about how you handle your areas of responsibility.

Something you cannot forget is to train and educate new employees in 5S. Everyone who has been a part of the process probably understands it, but that might not be the case for someone who has just been hired or who has been away for some time.

To easily maintain 5S, it has to be simple to understand what everyone is responsible for and how things are supposed to work. Visualize your standardized level with pictures, put up diagrams that show the results from audits, and celebrate improvement. Make instructions for everything, including 5S cards, checklists, calendars or policies, and make sure they are visible and easy to understand for outsiders. Schedule overviews and follow-ups of all the visualizations so that only valid information is up and old information is taken down.

Case study – Implement 5S in one week

Aditro is a leading Nordic software and service company that focuses on solutions and services for digitalized and automatized Human Resource Management. Aditro's products and services are used by middle-sized and large organizations and companies, and by the public sector. The company has 1,300 employees.

I spoke to Daniel Adolfson, Lean Expert, about their implementation of 5S at one unit, where approximately 100 employees work on digitalizing material.

OO: Why did you choose 5S as your work method?

DA: We started by making an extensive analysis and a detailed value-flow analysis that allowed us to study the value-flow. Our value-flow is:

Material in -> Sorting -> Opening -> Dividing into three value-flows -> Central scanning -> Back to the value-flows for digital verification

It turned out that the problem was not lead times, as the process was normally completed in less than a day. The overall problem was in the big differences in the workload during the month. The goal, therefore, became to even out the workload and run the facility with a long-term goal of achieving efficient and flexible staffing.

We chose 5S as a tool to visualize and create clear flows within the establishment.

Another reason for choosing 5S was that we saw it as a way to move forward with lean work, since

5S is essentially practical management and coworker training. It also gives positive effects connected to productivity and quality, which is always welcome.

OO: What did you do to get the managers and employees engaged?

DA: We started by creating a "change story" with the management where we discussed the current situation and possible future scenarios. This helped the managers communicate the plans with their coworkers.

Afterwards, we worked with the staff in workshops to discuss today's problems and possibilities. Something that came up often during the meetings was the lack of order. Together, we discussed what that means for us and how things should work instead. That allowed us to come up with real suggestions. As a complement to the conversations, we also created a goal image that described the goals that should be achieved with 5S in detail.

OO: How did you work practically with the change?

DA: We divided the unit into three parts and made a detailed plan for each part, which took half a year. The whole change took roughly 18 months and included more lean discipline than 5S. 5S was the initial step for all three improvement areas.

In the first improvement area, we began with a small and outlined pilot area. That way, everyone could see and learn what 5S was in a practical way. Following this, we put through a bigger implementation for the area.

In my experience, 5S cannot become a long-term project. Dragging the implementation out is a sure way to fail. We therefore worked in a concentrated way for one week in every area of the value-flow. It is important to identify the appropriately sized areas from the resources available. During the week, we had freed up enough time for the staff to participate. When possible, all of the staff from the field in question was with us. When that was not possible, we worked with appointed delegates. A reconciliation was done with the rest of the work team every morning so that everyone knew about the changes going on.

The most important thing was that the leaders were constantly involved. If they are not, 5S will not succeed. The order might be maintained for a short while, but long-term effects and the larger improvement work would not be possible.

Each day, we took a step further into 5S based on a detailed time schedule and also made improvements in practice. After a week, we were basically done. The remaining tasks we handled simultaneously with the audits being performed.

OO: How have you maintained and kept improving this way of working?

DA: The managers perform audits every week, along with a coworker. The following day, the results are presented together with deviations and suggestions for improvement are made. However, the main point is that the employees themselves should identify ways for improving on the deviations. In that way, the managers are more present and problems are taken care of right away.

Something important is to "celebrate success" when you have accomplished your goals. This can be done with something as simple as a "luxurious coffee break" or some fun common activities.

OO: What is important to consider in order to succeed with 5S?

DA: It is important to plant the "seeds" over time, especially among managers and leaders, but also with the informal leaders in the organization so that they have time to prepare for what is coming. Sometimes, you will have to make some tough decisions, in which case it is good if the leaders are prepared and understand the change. It is also good if the improvement leaders who support the implementation are well prepared, have a detailed plan, and have gathered vital information. This is necessary to avoid losing your focus during a fast implementation.

However, one of the most fundamental pillars is to create safety, knowledge, and understanding with the manager in charge of implementing 5S. They need to act as role models throughout the implementation.

OO: What results have you seen from 5S?

DA: What is most noticeable is that the employees now feel more pride in their workplace. There is a new kind of openness and efficient communication with the work teams. More responsibility is being taken, both from the teams and individually.

For the establishment, the most important result of 5S is that it is now possible for us to put other improvements into place in an efficient way. This is possible because the leaders have grown stronger and developed their knowledge, and the employees are starting to understand what it means to work towards a physical standard and handle deviations. The organization has achieved some fundamental cornerstones of knowledge and behavior, all of which are necessary to work towards efficient improvement work in the future.

5S has therefore made it possible for us to move forward and implement a standardized way of working, along with boosting performance management and establishing a system for developing competence.

With respect to the commercial aspect, productivity has increased, as the newly optimized work areas have rendered more efficient handling of the work assignments. The quality of the value-flow has improved. This is because clear and optimized workplaces simplify the job. It has become easier and faster to do things right.

OO: You also have some experience with Volvo; what do you think separates 5S in the service industry from the workshop industry?

DA: The interest in order already exists on both sides. Within the production industry, it may be easier to see the direct gain of 5S, since you often have a lot of physical material to handle there. However, I think that the gain is significant in both places, even if it is harder to measure in the service industry. Often, a lot of time disappears in the office environment, for example, because of the print room. It is very common to have significant waste connected to the printer, which might be out of paper or toner, may require simple maintenance instructions, or even a missing phone number for technical support. This can be eliminated by using 5S. The same thing goes for office necessities. Here, you can save a lot of money by structuring the cabinets and identifying simple re-ordering points, which can make the purchase process more efficient.

Something to think about when implementing 5S within an industry is to connect 5S to operator maintenance or preventive maintenance. Then, the total effect will be bigger than if you implement them separately.

Implementing and roles

Is 5S a project?

Is 5S a temporary project or an ongoing change that is never really finished? The answer is...both.

The implementing of 5S can definitely be seen as a project. It has clear goals (implementing the five steps on a time schedule), requires resources to succeed, cross-functional cooperation is necessary, and proper planning is essential.

5S is not an investment project, where a smaller group works independently and then hands their work over to a recipient. 5S is best described as a "change project," where, ideally, all of the employees participate in various ways from the beginning, with the common goal of succeeding.

Who is leading the change?

Sometimes, 5S change is only driven by ordinary management, without support from internal or external experts and resource professionals. The upside to this is that anchoring and maintaining 5S becomes natural. The downside is that the change can take a painfully long time, as you might only work with 5S when the situation allows for it.

At other times, 5S is driven by a staff organization on a direct request from a higher manager. The upside to this is that resources are readily available and there is the capacity for fast results. The downside is the challenge of getting real anchoring and ownership with the participating managers.

The most successful examples have found a balance where the managers take part of the responsibility for implementing and maintaining, but where a supporting organization is also involved with the education, planning and standardizing during the implementation process.

The following roles are common during implementation. In a smaller organization, the same person can have different roles, while in a big organization there could be many of the same kind.

Responsible managing

As the manager, you cannot delegate the improvement work.

It is fine to delegate and get help with different practical parts of the 5S work, such as educating, creating visualization boards, and writing 5S-cards.

What cannot be delegated, however, is the stubbornness and dedication that is demanded from you as a manager to change the culture of the company.

> You cannot delegate the improvement work

The good news is that pretty much everyone wants order, and if you perform the five steps in the right way, the staff will have been a key part of creating the routines and the standards.

Remember, this does not mean that the change will fall into place without any conflict!

There will always be differing opinions on the details. One area will be how the responsibility and workload should be divided. When you have finally decided about which standard you want and what routines are going to work, this has to be followed, even if some people do not agree on everything.

Another important consideration is setting a good example. What does it look like in your own office? Implement 5S there as part of the overall implementation. In that way, you get a feeling of what changes 5S really requires and you can answer questions more adequately.

Let 5S be part of the judgment during performance reviews and salary discussions. Let a potential hire's attitude towards order be a factor when you are recruiting new people. This should be seen as part of the work skills being evaluated.

An un-prioritized 5S routine is a debt

As a leader, you sometimes have to prioritize other things besides cleaning. We are supposed to always protect the client and cannot do everything according to our initial plans. As a manager, you should consider this de-prioritization as a debt that needs to be repaid.

For example, it is fine to say, "We need to fill this truck now to make the delivery, so we will clean Tuesday morning instead of today like we planned." The most important thing is that 5S is not seen as something you only do when you have time.

(The need for re-planning should be seen as a deviation. If it is repeated, improvement work should be initiated.)

Responsible team leadership

As a team leader, you have a big responsibility to ensure that 5S works in practice. To do this, you must firstly know what should be done, as well as when and how. Many times, the team leader ensures that all the 5S tasks are finished on time; they are also responsible for introducing the appropriate way of working to new employees.

To help you, you have the 5S visualization board, where you can see clearly what responsibilities your team has, how everything should look, all of the required routines, and a checklist or some other method for follow ups so that you easily can see what should be done, by whom, and when it was last completed.

Another important tool is the weekly audit system, which the team leaders often perform themselves. Here, you have to consider all deviations and initiate changes in the standards and routines when needed. A good question to ask is, "Is there anything stopping us from following our routines?" If there is something hindering you, then it is your duty to make sure that it is resolved, with help from your other team members or with help from support organizations.

When needed, bring up problems with resources or motivation with higher managers as soon as possible.

I usually compare the team leaders' role with how the cabin crew of an airplane makes sure that every passenger is following the safety instructions. Before every flight, the stewards/steward-esses go through all security details and instruct passengers on how to act. Before takeoff, you put on your seatbelt and follow other instructions. Deviations in this situation are handled in a certain way. If someone refused to listen, the captain would be contacted to handle the situation.

Similarly, the team leader should train, instruct and profession-ally ensure that everything works. If that is not possible, then you should initiate work for improvement.

Responsible higher management

If you are part of the higher management, then it is important to understand your role in the 5S work. Invest time in understand-ing the new way of working so that you see the potential and are aware of what changes are going to occur.

One approach to this is to participate in education along with other staff so that you fully understand 5S and hear what people have to say about it. Nothing is as bad for motivation as a higher manager thinking that 5S is only about cleaning up, particularly when every other employee is properly trained and understands the big picture.

Speak with internal or external experts to better understand the need for resources and make an extensive plan for several years where 5S is incorporated into other improvement initiatives. Even if it is hard to make a proper investment template for 5S, the direct and indirect effects can be estimated and must be compared to the expenses.

For example, in a production environment, you can expect increased maintenance expenses during the implementation phase, since an unusually high number of problems might come up and need to be resolved. The gain is demonstrated through increased productivity, increased possibility, implementing other improvements, and a workplace that can be shown to clients and investors with pride.

During the implementation phase, the higher management should be aware of how plans are put through and prioritized and establish a regular dialogue with the employees. They should participate in quarterly/yearly audits and encourage groups with diplomas in 5S. They should also make sure that job descriptions, job ads, or payment systems are updated so that maintaining 5S becomes an integrated part of every manager's normal work.

One way to simplify the implementation within a bigger organization is to express and communicate in a company policy the way to handle order and cleanliness.

For example:

- "A clean, safe and well working factory is good for us and our customers."

- "Maintaining order is a natural part of work for all employees."

This policy then becomes part of your company policy or part of your production system.

The purpose of the policy is to give your staff something to lean on when making decisions. For example, is it okay to give someone a day off, despite some 5S assignments not being finished? What is more important, keeping the place clean or decreasing overtime?

Internal or external 5S experts

To succeed, you may need the help of a 5S expert. This person could come from your own organization, perhaps because they have been part of a successful implementation before, or it could be an external consultant. If you choose to work internally, think about how it might be hard to be an expert and part of the work team at the same time.

The usual role of the expert:

- Trains the staff in 5S. In a large organization, you may choose to use the expert to train your trainers instead.

- Helps share educational material, informational material, visualization boards, checklists, etc.

- Coaches everyone involved on their respective parts in each step. You can never fully copy someone else's solution; you have to develop your own details based on your own conditions. Do not be scared to challenge habits and normal ways of working. If no changes were needed, the work would be unnecessary.

I think that the expert's goal should be to make themselves unnecessary as soon as possible. Here's an example from a larger factory where I was actually hired as a "5S expert." By the implementation phase, they chose to divide the establishment into three parts. The first six months, they implemented 5S in the first chosen third of the company. At that point, I led the training for all employees and the coaching at all the steps for key people.

In the next six months, it was time for the next step. This time, the factory staff did practically everything themselves. I only visited them two times to discuss certain problems that had arisen.

In the last third of the project, they managed themselves completely without external help. After completing the first factory, their internal project manager is now regularly hired as an internal consultant at other factories in that company.

The 5S leader

In a larger organization where multiple 5S initiatives can be put through at the same time, you should appoint someone to look at the big picture. I usually call him/her the "5S leader." Other names are the WCM-Champion, Lean Manager, etc. The goal is that the 5S leader should be able to take over from the external expert to work as an internal consult in the future.

The 5S leader is responsible for:

- Planning the work so that no resources run out. For example, the maintenance department can get overloaded if everyone starts coming in with demands to fix something because of the 5S work.

- Providing information to the organization. Even if everyone will not be involved with the 5S work at the same time, everyone needs to understand what is going on and when/how it is going to affect them. This is done by informational meetings, intra networks, and other similar approaches.

- Setting standards for 5S boards and visualizations. To make it simpler for others, it is best if there are as many finished templates as possible (even if there has to be some flexibility depending on your conditions).

- Creating visualization boards that show how far the 5S work has come along in different areas.

- Creating diplomas and overseeing the audits for diplomas in workplaces.

- After a while, take over the consultant's role for training and coaching.

5S coach

One or several 5S coaches should be appointed for every work team, depending on the team size. They perform a lot of the practical work, such as creating and updating 5S cards, fixing boards, booking audits or training.

In a larger organization with several 5S coaches, it is important that they get the chance to meet on a regular basis to coordinate the work along with the 5S leader and the managers of the organization.

Planning the work

The time it takes to implement 5S is dependent on various factors, such as how big the areas are that you are going to work with, the number of people involved, how big of a cultural change it will mean and how many resources are available in the form of support and experts. In most cases, each should not take longer than a month. If it is hard to keep up, you should divide the implementation into even smaller units.

Should you initially try out a pilot area or work with the whole establishment from the beginning? The upside with a pilot area is that you can learn the way of working and start creating standardized templates. The downside is that the work team within the pilot area will be ahead of everyone else. You will need to handle the various levels of understanding of the concept and even different cultures within the company.

If you choose to work with a pilot, pick the right department to start in. Implementation demands certain resources, so you should begin working where the pay-off is shortest and where the effect will be clear. Invest properly to set a good example, but assure the other employees that the work will soon include them as well.

To implement 5S in a bigger workplace, a plan like the one below (image 29) is appropriate. In this example, the estimate is that every step will take one month. After five months, the first group will be done.

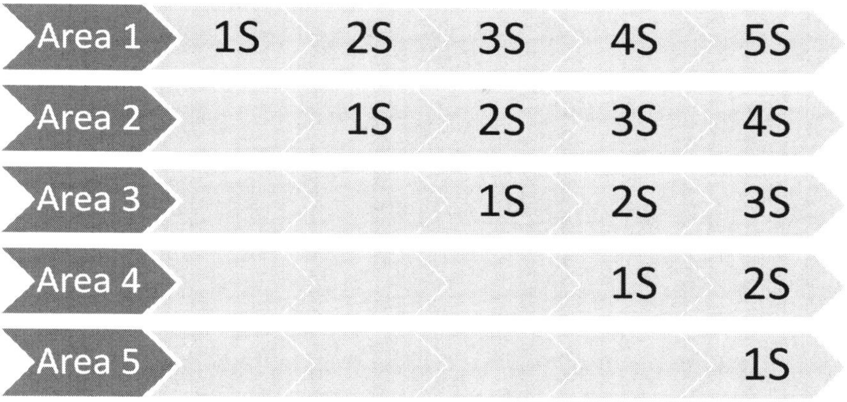

Area 1	1S	2S	3S	4S	5S
Area 2		1S	2S	3S	4S
Area 3			1S	2S	3S
Area 4				1S	2S
Area 5					1S

Image 29. Example of a 5S roll-out plan

Training

A necessary component for successful implementation is training in 5S. The training should include all staff members that spend their time in the affected area. For example, in a production plant, the operators, maintenance staff, managers and technicians should all be involved.

It is also important for the participants learning the 5S theory to be allowed to discuss common questions in the work team and create an understanding that everyone actually wants order.

Visualization

Put up your 5S visualization board early in the process. In the beginning of the work, these boards will mainly be used for project information, plans, organization of action plans and so on. This work is intended to establish order in your workplace, so make sure the board looks good and clean from the start.

During the implementation, the boards will gradually become a tool to support the maintenance of 5S. The board should eventually visualize standards for how everything should look, as well as how the work, improvement, and follow-ups should be done. Adjust the size of the board according to what you will eventually need to include on it.

When the work is finished, the board will act as a small quality management system that you use to run daily activities.

You can see a good example of a board on image 9.

Planning for Step One - Sorting

All of the staff should participate in this step. It is best if the staff in the workplace are divided into cross-functional work teams that together mark flaws with red tags in the facility and sort material into different piles.

Everything that makes the cleaning harder or makes things dirty should be fixed. The same goes for all kinds of known faults and uncomfortable work duties that steal time from your day. Every unnecessary item should be removed.

As a 5S leader, it is important to be active and point out things that the group might have missed. Bring a new perspective so that everyone can learn to look at things differently.

Every solution is collected into a plan of action to be performed throughout the workplace. Your goal should be to get rid of all of the red tags within 30 days.

Planning for Step Two - Organizing

During this step, it is common to work with representatives from the different workplaces – the 5S coaches. Begin the Organizing Step when most of the actions from the Sorting Step have been finished. Do not think about simply placing tools and other things in the right place; also work to create visually pleasing workplaces with clear and efficient flows.

Planning for Step Three – Cleaning

This step should be conducted by the entire staff, as this is when you decide on a common standard and suggest which routines should be maintained in the future. It also boosts motivation when everyone is included.

Remember to point out that there are two important goals with the initial cleanse besides simply cleaning. One is to jointly agree on what level of cleanliness you think is proper; the other goal is to document what was needed to reach this new level, which provides input for establishing new routines.

Plan the cleaning carefully. Make sure that you have all necessary equipment ready. The initial cleanse is best done in teams. Bring out a documentation template and let the teams estimate how often each cleaning should be done in the future, and how much time it would take if done regularly. Finish by photographing the new standard.

Appoint people to oversee the dirt that comes back daily and document potential sources.

Planning for Step Four – Routines

This is the most critical stage of 5S. Once you create the routine, you will benefit from the documentation that was done during the cleaning step.

If it was done well, then you already know what routines are needed and you can estimate how much time they will take.

To make sure that the level from the initial cleaning is not lost, the new routines should be put in place as soon as possible. Many times, it can be good to start with a simple, temporary system for routines, such as a paper-based system or Post-It notes on a white board, while you are building a more permanent and visual system, such as a board for 5S cards.

The production of 5S cards or checklists is normally completed by the 5S coaches.

Planning for Step 5 - Discipline

This is what ties the different parts together. The goal is to make 5S a natural part of the daily work process and create conditions that enable this new way of working to grow and evolve.

Remember that even the best routines can fail if the managers do not consistently demonstrate how important they are. Follow-ups should never be a task "if we can find the time." Create an audit system and schedule regular audits.

Help the management by visualizing responsibilities, routines, and follow-ups. An effective tool for this is the creation of a certification system, in addition to following how far the different departments have come on public boards.

The next step – Connect 5S to the improvement work

Everything we have implemented with 5S has to be updated, improved, and adjusted to constantly changing realities. This includes routines, standards, responsibilities, boards, flows, rewards, etc.

The goal is not only to keep everything clean and nice; it should also become simpler over time to maintain the standard you have set.

Use the audits as a way to encourage improvement proposals. During the audits, it is wise to ask questions, including:

- Does anything you are doing at work feel unnecessary or difficult?

- What could be improved?

- Do we always follow our work instructions? If not, what is hindering us?

- Are there any safety risks while working?

- Is something heavy or hard to do?

It is important that documenting all the problems or suggestions that arise is simple. Also, you need a process for handling suggestions or problems quickly. For example, bring them up at weekly meetings and implement a simple method of visualizing every errand and its decision-making stage. This performance process should be communally shared so that everyone can see where "their" suggestion is.

Appendix 1 Example

Audit form

	1	2	3	4	5
All unnecessary things have been cleared out of the workplace					
All temporary solutions (of the tape and steel wire variety) are permanently fixed					
There are no safety risks while working					
Everything we use regularly is available in marked places					
Floor markings, transportation avenues, surfaces, etc. have been marked					
We do not need to repeatedly bend our backs, lift, or move unnecessarily heavy things as part of our daily work					
It is easy to keep things clean (no loose items on the floor or workplace, etc.)					
We have eliminated all the main sources of dirt					
There is a commonly agreed standard of how clean the workplace should be, such as through pictures					

We have clear cleaning routines to maintain the agreed-upon standard					
All routines are performed according to an agreed-upon system					
There are responsible people for all tool boards and similar elements of the system					
5S-audits are performed regularly based on an agreed schedule					
Every level of management is engaged in 5S					
A certification system shows which workplaces have reached an approved 5S level					